Birds in Winter

Marc Duquet

Illustrations
François Desbordes
and
Jean Chevallier
Denis Clavreul
Fernand Mognetti

Translated by
Jo Weightman

HarperCollins*Publishers*

COLLINS WATCH GUIDES

Black and white artwork: Alban
Larousse
Translation: Jo Weightman

ISBN 0 00 220100 3
©Éditions Gallimard, Paris, 1995
© in this translation HarperCollins*Publishers*, London, 1997
Printed and bound in Italy

Contents

Birds and Winter

Winter is a critical time for birds. Food becomes scarce when the weather is cold and snow lies on the ground. Survival is difficult, so millions of birds migrate southwards in late summer. This is why many of the species that can be seen during winter in Britain are different from those seen in the summer.

● The **brambling** reaches Britain in October and departs March–April.

Brambling

Some birds which breed in summer in the far north of Europe fly south to spend the winter with us (1). These include brambling, redwing and many species of duck.

Some forms of the white-fronted goose, brent geese, knot and turnstone which spend the winter in western Europe come from North America and Greenland (2)

● Tits, nuthatches, chaffinches and even great spotted woodpeckers, which are woodland birds, come close to houses in winter.

Before the onset of winter, storks, swallows, warblers and swifts set off from Europe on a long flight to Africa where they overwinter in a warmer climate (3)

Swallow

● The **wallcreeper** spends the winter on cliffs in valleys.

● In common with some other European birds, the **house sparrow**, blackbird and dunnock are primarily resident, that is, they spend the whole year in the same area.

House sparrow

Most mountain birds, such as the wallcreeper and the alpine accentor, spend the winter down in the valleys (5).

❹

Thousands of rooks, lapwings and fieldfares arrive from Russia and eastern Europe to spend the winter in western Europe (4).

7

Some bird species travel short distances (6).

When they leave Europe at the end of the summer, white storks either go via the Straits of Gibraltar or over the Bosphorus in order to avoid flying over the Mediterranean (7).

● During the winter, **blue tits** come close to houses to look for food.

Winter Plumage

White undertail coverts

Red bill with a yellow tip

White line on the flanks

Green legs

Feathery base to the bill

Square-ended tail

● In late summer and autumn, the attractive white line on the flanks of the **moorhen** often fades as the feathers age. At the same time, its plumage becomes brownish.

● The plumage of the **carrion crow** remains black all over in summer and winter. However, in late summer the worn feathers take on a slightly brown tint.

White wing patch

Male

Red below the tail

● The **great spotted woodpecker** has the same black, white and red plumage all year round. The male can be distinguished from the female by the red nape-patch.

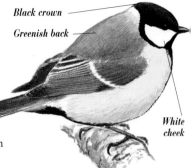

Black crown

Greenish back

White cheek

● The **great tit** has the same brightly coloured plumage all year round. In early spring the feathers are most worn and the plumage is more dull.

A bird's fragile feathers become worn and have to be renewed regularly. When they moult, some species exchange their dull winter colours for brilliant breeding plumage. Others have plumage which is almost the same all year round.

● In winter, the brownish tips to the new feathers often mask the olive-green colour of the **greenfinch's** plumage. In spring, these wear away, revealing yellow tones.

Yellow wing and tail patches

Summer Plumage

Black head and back

Bright chestnut breast

Black bill

Black crown

White collar

White moustachial stripe and black bib

● The male **brambling** displays its breeding colours, a characteristic glossy black on the head and back, when it is on its northern breeding grounds. These colours may also often be seen in spring before the species leaves Britain.

● In spring, the male **reed bunting** in breeding plumage can be distinguished from the female by its black head and white moustachial stripe. The plumage of the female resembles the male's winter colours.

Brown-black head

Dark red bill and legs

Chestnut crown and upperparts

Long, somewhat curved bill

Black belly patch

● The **black-headed gull** sometimes acquires the brown-black cap of its breeding plumage by mid-winter. During the breeding season, the bill and legs are a darker colour.

● In summer, the **dunlin** is reddish-brown with a characteristic black patch on the belly. It breeds in upland Britain but huge numbers also arrive from the north for the winter.

Bright yellow bill

Black crest

Chestnut collar

Dark bill

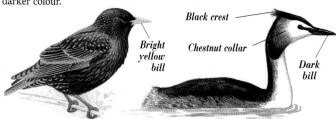

● The **starling** in breeding plumage is black with numerous metallic crimson and green speckles. The bill is yellow.

● When in breeding plumage, the **great crested grebe** has a tufted crest on the back of its head and a wide, black-edged, chestnut collar.

Bar-tailed godwit

Snow bunting

Dunlin

Spotted redshank

● During June and July, the **dunlin**, **spotted redshank**, **bar-tailed godwit** and **snow bunting** display the bright, contrasting colours of their plumage against the Arctic tundra, somewhere in the far north of Scandinavia (see above).

● A few months later, these species are once more side by side many hundreds of kilometres further south. Their winter plumage is then much less brilliant, so much so that it is hard to imagine they are the same birds (see below).

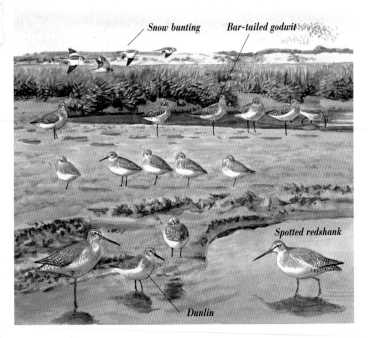

Snow bunting

Bar-tailed godwit

Spotted redshank

Dunlin

Birdwatching: Where to Go

● In winter, birds often find shelter in gardens, both private and public. Householders or visitors often put out food: breadcrumbs, sunflower seeds etc.

Birds which winter in western Europe are mainly found in the lowlands and at the coast where the climate is mildest. In such places there are large undisturbed areas where huge numbers of ducks, geese, waders and passerine birds gather.

Small birds can find food in vegetable patches near built-up areas during winter

Birds often come into towns and villages to combat severe winter weather

Woodland birds, such as chaffinches, gather with larks on stubble fields and ploughed land in winter

Mud banks in estuaries provide food and shelter for numerous waders and other water birds

Chestnut shoulder

White rump

Chestnut wing bar

Yellow, black-tipped bill

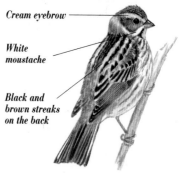

Cream eyebrow

White moustache

Black and brown streaks on the back

● When the **brambling** reaches Britain in early winter it has new plumage. The feathers of the crown and back have creamy brown tips, masking the black, but the chestnut breast and white rump are characteristic.

● Like most buntings, the **reed bunting** has much duller plumage in winter than in summer. After the post-breeding moult, the new feathers are edged with creamy brown, making the plumage look rather drab.

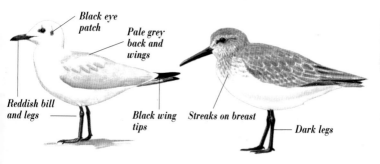

Black eye patch

Pale grey back and wings

Reddish bill and legs

Black wing tips

Streaks on breast

Dark legs

● The winter plumage of the **black-headed gull** is very little different from the summer plumage. However, the head totally changes colour. In winter, it is white with a small black patch behind the eye.

● In winter, the plumage of the **dunlin** is altogether different from its breeding plumage. It is hard to see that this is the same species. Many small waders are white and greyish in winter.

Dark bill

Numerous white specks

Black crown

Black line joining the eye and bill

Pink, dagger-shaped bill

● The **starling** has black plumage with close creamy-white speckles in winter. The pale tips of the new feathers will gradually wear away during the winter, revealing the breeding colours in early spring.

● In winter, the **great crested grebe** has dull plumage, appearing black and white from a distance. As the season progresses, long coloured feathers grow on its head, forming the main feature of the breeding plumage of this species.

● In winter, brackish habitats such as coastal lagoons attract birds.

● Coastal grasslands and saltmarshes are very attractive to geese and plover.

● Redwing, song thrush and blackbirds can find berries in abundance in traditionally managed hedges.

Slow-moving rivers often support ducks when still water is frozen

Meadows attract flocks of fieldfare, lapwing and golden plover. Hen harriers often hunt here.

● Rarer ducks are often hidden among large flocks of tufted duck and pochard.

Fairly large patches of water are favourite gathering grounds for ducks, coot and grebe

Small insect-eating birds may find enough to keep them alive during the winter on wooded hillsides

Nuthatch and Tits

Blue crown

Yellow underparts

Black line

● **Blue tits** look like small, plump great tits. They can be recognised, however, by their blue crown and wings.

Tits are common around houses in winter although they are primarily woodland birds the rest of the year. They are often joined by nuthatches which like to take advantage of the food people put out for birds.

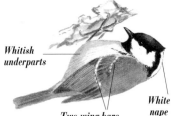

Whitish underparts

Two wing bars

White nape

● The **coal tit**, which is black and white only, can be recognised by the white patch on its nape and two white wing bars.

● In winter, tits move about in flocks seeking food.

● The **willow tit** differs from the marsh tit by its slightly rounder silhouette and the rather spreading, badly defined black chin patch.

Short tail

● The **nuthatch** lives in trees, often perching head downwards. The bluish upperparts and buff underparts are characteristic.

Powerful bill

Pale patch on the wing

Brownish patch behind the cheek

Wing all one colour

● The **crested tit** has a black crown streaked with white and a characteristic black mark behind the eye and cheek. It occasionally ventures into gardens.

● The **marsh tit** looks larger and more slender than the willow tit. The black bib is small and clearly defined.

● In winter, the tiny **lesser spotted woodpecker** visits urban trees and gardens. Both male (red crown) and female have black upperparts with white stripes. It has a flight pattern like a tit.

Willow tit

● **Blue tits** are real acrobats and will hang upside down to take seeds.

Nuthatch

● The **great tit** will venture right onto a window sill but the nuthatch keeps its distance, preferring a vertical perch.

Blue tit

● The **great tit** is the largest of the tits. The characteristic smart black 'tie' on its yellow breast is wider in the male than in the female.

Black crown
White cheeks

Black stripe on belly

Yellow underparts

Finches

Greenfinch

The great majority of finches and their relatives are seed eaters. They can therefore survive the winter so long as the snow is not too deep to prevent them finding food. They come readily to food put out in winter and are very fond of sunflower seeds.

The brambling can be easily picked out in flocks of chaffinches by its pure white rump

Female

Double white wing bar

Male

● Although less bright than in summer, the blue and pink plumage of the male **chaffinch** is still visible in winter. The double white wing bar is characteristic.

Male

Blackish head

Female

● The **brambling** can be distinguished from the chaffinch by its blackish head and rusty breast and shoulders. The female is less brightly coloured than the male.

● In winter, **redpoll** (red forehead and black-streaked plumage) flock with **siskin** (yellow streaked with black) to feed on birch and alder seed.

● Like the siskin, the **greenfinch** has yellow-green plumage but is more uniformly coloured, lacking dark streaks, and is a larger bird.

Wing edged with yellow

Yellow patches on the tail

Goldfinch

Great tit

Chaffinch

Greenfinch

● The **greenfinch**, an aggressive bird, will not allow other birds to feed with it at a bird table. The others perch on the roof waiting their turn.

● Notice the stout beaks of the finches – ideal for crushing seeds.

● Chaffinches and greenfinches are the commonest finches in gardens in winter. From November to March they are joined by brambling when severe weather prevents these from finding food in the fields.

Large conical bill

The hawfinch emits a sharp 'tsic' in flight

White wing bar

Short, white-bordered tail

● The **bullfinch** feeds largely on buds and causes a lot of damage to garden shrubs in spring. Its black crown and pink underside are charateristic, although the female is duller.

● The **hawfinch,** easily recognised by its huge conical bill and wide white wing bar, sometimes comes into gardens in winter.

13

Thrushes, Blackbirds

Bright chestnut flanks

White eyebrow

Streaked breast

Redwing eating rowan berries

Thrushes, blackbirds and the robin belong to the Turdidae, a family which feeds on earthworms and fruit in winter. Redwings and fieldfares spend the summer in the far north as a rule and fly south to Britain for the winter. While the robin is territorial and solitary in winter, thrushes flock in fields, sometimes in large numbers, and blackbirds gather in small groups.

● The **redwing** can be recognised by its chestnut flanks and white eye-line. It can often be seen among flocks of fieldfares and song thrushes.

Mistle thrush: white underwing and white outer tail tips. Flight call: *trrrree*.

Fieldfare: white underwing. Flight call: *tchac-tchac*.

Song thrush: buff underwing. Flight call: *tic*.

Redwing: bright chestnut underwing. Flight call: *tssib*.

● The **fieldfare** is a large, very colourful thrush: the head and rump are grey, the breast rather rusty, speckled with black, the back red-brown and the bill yellow with a black tip.

Pale, grey-brown colours

Dark brown and white pattern on the wing

Large, round, dark spots

Grey head

Chestnut-brown back

Yellow base to the bill

● The **mistle thrush** looks like a large song thrush with pale, grey-brown plumage. The wings are strongly marked with a dark brown and white pattern.

and Robins

Female

● The female **blackbird** is dark brown with a pale patch under the throat. The bill is dark.

Wing entirely brown

● Look closely at the flocks of **fieldfare** in the fields. Sometimes they are accompanied by mistle thrushes and redwings.

● Everyone knows the **robin** with its bright orange face and throat. In winter, it prefers to eat earthworms and other small creatures rather than fruit.

Orange throat and cheeks

Breast flushed with cream

White belly

● The **song thrush** has rather unstriking plumage, dull brown above and white speckled with black beneath. It is found everywhere, including towns.

Robin

● In winter, the **blackbird** feeds mostly on fruit. The male's wholly black plumage, yellow bill and long tail distinguish it from the starling (see page 7).

Male blackbird

In Towns

In winter, many birds find shelter in towns where the temperature is higher than in the open countryside and more food is available. Towns situated on rivers are therefore popular with gulls, while ducks enjoy the shelter offered by ornamental pools and lakes in public gardens where the water is not frozen.

Black and white plumage

Long, gradually tapering tail

● Once a bird of the countryside, the **magpie** now nests in tall trees in towns as well.

Cream eye stripe

Striped back

Grey crown

Chestnut wing

Stout bill

Male

Female

● The **house sparrow** is always to be found where there are people, feeding on scraps of food. The female is less brightly coloured than the male.

● **Black-headed gulls**, birds of lakes and marshland, are often common in winter along rivers.

● The male **house sparrow** is paler in winter than in spring: later on, as his feathers get old, brighter colours are revealed.

Herring gull in a flock of black-headed gulls

● The **dunnock** is a shy bird, feeding on the ground under bushes. It resembles a female sparrow but has grey-blue underparts.

Back brown with black streaks

Slender bill   Dunnock

● **Blackbirds** (left) hop while **starlings** (right) walk. In winter, the starling has characteristic white speckles on its plumage. Starlings also have much shorter tails.

Canada geese, which have been introduced into Britain from North America, can be seen in some urban parks but also in the open countryside.

White cheeks

Long black neck

● Herring gulls and lesser black-backed gulls come up rivers, sometimes far inland.

Mallard ducks

Starling roosts are very noisy at dusk

Coot and Grebe

Cormorants perch in dead trees, which are whitened by their droppings

● The **great crested grebe** has a long neck and a dagger-shaped bill. Wide white wing patches are conspicuous in flight.

Stretches of freshwater with tall vegetation at the edges are good places for great crested grebe, little grebe and coot. In winter they are joined by cormorants and other species of grebe. These species stay out in the open water where they are easy to watch.

When seen flying in the distance, cormorants may be mistaken for geese or cranes. They have a characteristic cross-shaped silhouette.

Cormorant

Coot

Great crested grebe

F.Desbordes

Red, yellow-tipped bill

White on the tail

● **Moorhens** look like coots but have a red bill with a yellow tip and white on the flanks and under the tail.

● The **great crested grebe's** breeding colours appear in mid-winter. Chestnut at the back of the head brightens up its brown and white plumage.

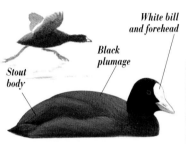

White bill and forehead

Black plumage

Stout body

● When taking flight, the **coot** runs along the surface of the water.

● The **black-necked grebe** has black and white plumage in winter, a plump silhouette and a slightly up-turned bill.

Coot often stay in close flocks

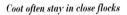

Cormorant

Coot

Black crown

Black line joining the eye and bill

Brownish plumage

The little grebe dives frequently

Small size

Male mallard

Dabbling Ducks

Dabbling ducks feed at the surface by sticking their heads into the water or by up-ending so that only the tail end is visible. They do not dive. The males are mostly brightly coloured, but the females are all brown, flecked with black. The mallard is the commonest of the six species seen in Britain in winter. Dabbling ducks take off by leaping into the air.

Mallard: blue-purple speculum

Gadwall: white speculum

Shoveler: wing blue above

Pintail: needle tail

Black eye-line
Orange spot on the bill
Female
Male

Wigeon: wing white above

Teal: very small with green speculum

Long, flattened bill
Female
Male

● The male **mallard** can be recognised by its bottle-green head, chestnut-brown breast, grey body and bright yellow bill.

● The bright chestnut flanks of the male **shoveler** contrast with its white body, bottle-green head and yellow eyes.

Female
Yellow edge to the bill
Male

Blue-grey bill
Female
Male

● The male **gadwall** has dull plumage: the body is grey with a black rump and a white patch on the wing.

● The **pintail** is a slender, elegant bird. Characteristic features of the male are its white neck, brown head and long tail.

Wigeon

The white upper wing and belly of the wigeon are very obvious when in flight

Gadwall

Pintail

Females are often accompanied by one or more males. (These are shovelers.)

When the wigeon is on land, the white belly can be seen

● Surface ducks readily feed on land and usually dabble in shallow water, not far from the bank.

Teal: yellow under the tail, white line on the flanks

● The golden-yellow forehead of the **wigeon** can be seen from far off. It is in marked contrast to the chestnut head of this pale, grey-bodied species. The female is brown with a small bluish-grey bill.

● From a distance, the little **teal** appears dark all over. Close to, the green eye patch and brown head of the male can be seen. Male and female both have a green speculum which is often visible.

Diving Ducks

Diving ducks disappear completely under the water while they seek food on the bottom. They have heavy bodies and have to run along the water surface to take off. Tufted duck and pochard are typical examples. Goosander and smew, as well as goldeneye, occur in smaller numbers in the winter.

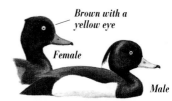

Brown with a yellow eye

Female

Male

● The male **tufted duck** is black with white flanks and yellow eyes. It has a long, drooping crest on its purplish head.

Female

White band at the base of the bill

Male

● **Scaup**, primarily maritime ducks, are quite rare inland. Males differ from tufted duck in their grey backs.

● The male **goldeneye** is black and white with a shiny green head and a white patch in front of the yellow eye.

Cream eye-line and base of bill

Female

Male

● The male **pochard** has a chocolate-brown head, black breast and grey body.

Scaup

Tufted duck

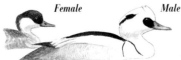

Pochard

Tufted duck

- In flight, **pochard** can be distinguished by the brown head and grey wing with a paler band further back.

- The white wing bar of the **tufted duck** contrasts strongly with the rest of the black plumage (apart from the belly).

Female   *Male*

Female   *Male*

- The male **smew** has white plumage with black markings. The female is grey with white cheeks and brown crown.

- The **goosander** is white with a bottle-green head and long, thin, red bill. The female has a pure white throat.

- Diving ducks may occupy deep waters like lakes and often gather out in the middle.

- Diving ducks (**pochard** on the left) can feed in deeper water than the surface-feeding ducks (**mallard** on the right).

Smew

Pochard

Geese and Swans

Flocks of Bewick swans may include several hundred individuals

In winter, the low-lying fields and grazing marshes in northwest Europe (especially in Britain and Holland) are home to thousands of geese and swans from Arctic regions. At this time of year, flocks of white-fronted and barnacle geese criss-cross the sky and the air is full of their honking. These winter visitors are joined by Bewick and whooper swans.

Greylag goose

Mute swan

● In flight, geese can be seen to have fairly long necks and short tails.

● Swans differ from geese in having a very long neck.

Bluish-grey upperparts

Short black bill with a pink patch

Dark brown upperparts

Black bill with an orange patch

Fairly long neck

Pink legs

Orange legs

● The **pink-footed goose** resembles the bean goose but is more compact. The dark head contrasts with the bluish-grey back and pinkish-brown breast. It overwinters mainly in Scotland, England, Belgium and Holland.

● The heavier **bean goose** has a longer neck than the pink-footed goose, dark brown upperparts, a rather long bill and orange legs. In winter, it usually gathers in small flocks throughout most of Europe.

Geese always fly in a V formation

Juvenile white-fronted goose

Greylag geese: heavy orange (or pinkish-orange) bill

F. Desbordes

● The **white-fronted goose** is characterised by a white ring at the base of the bill and black belly patches. Juvenile birds are grey-brown and have a small pink bill.

White ring   *Black belly patches*   *Adult white-fronted goose*

● The **greylag goose**, ancestor of the farmyard goose, is a large bird: it has a heavy orange bill and pink legs.

The barnacle is a small goose with black and grey plumage. Identifying features are the creamy-white face and black neck.

Orange bill with a black knob at the base

Rounded yellow patch at the base of the bill

Bill with wide, triangular yellow patch

Mute swan

Bewick swan

Whooper swan

● All three species of swan have entirely white plumage when adult. Juveniles are brownish-grey.

● The **mute swan** holds its neck in an 'S', **Bewick** and **whooper swans** have straight necks.

Sea Birds

Large numbers of birds shelter every winter on the coast, particularly in bays and estuaries. To the usual coastal species such as herring gull, cormorant and shelduck are added waders and ducks which have come down from the north.

● The **eider** is a Scandinavian bird with a characteristic strong, triangular bill. The male is black and white, the female brown barred with black.

Long curved bill

● The **curlew** often gathers in small flocks. Its black and brown speckled plumage gives it good camouflage.

Brownish head

Female

Male

● The male **red-breasted merganser** is very brightly coloured: dark green head, bright red beak, white collar, chestnut breast, grey and black body.

Curlew in flight

White rump

Male

Red knob on the bill

● **Shelduck** appear black and white from a distance but have a bottle-green head, chestnut foreparts and a red bill.

Black head and neck
White patch (adult)

● The **cormorant** has a hooked bill adapted for catching fish.

Cross-shaped silhouette

White patch

● From a distance, the **brent goose** appears to be black all over with white under the tail.

White chin and cheeks

● The **herring gull** is one of the commonest seaside birds. It keeps its silvery-grey mantle all year round but its head is streaked with brown in winter. The adult bird has a yellow bill with a red spot (darker during the winter).

Black wing tip

Silver-grey wings and back

White tail

● **Cormorants** live on the coast but also come inland where they may be very abundant in winter. At this time, the adult lacks the white patch on the thigh. Juveniles are black-brown with whitish underparts.

Flock of oystercatchers

Long straight bill

● **Oystercatchers** are common on seashores everywhere. They are black and white with a long, red bill and pink legs. In winter the bird has a white collar.

Black head and upperparts

Birds on Farmland

During harsh weather, larks, crows and lapwings gather in flocks on ploughed land and stubble fields in search of seed, insects and earthworms. Flocking together is also a good way to protect themselves against predators.

Chocolate-brown crown

Black patch

White cheeks

● The **tree sparrow** is more a bird of the countryside than the house sparrow from which it differs by its chocolate-brown crown and white cheeks with a small black patch. In winter it can be found in small flocks in hedges and stubble fields.

Short, rounded crest

● When feeding in flocks in fields, the **skylark** is well camouflaged by its brown, black-flecked plumage. In flight, the hindparts of the wing and tail margins show white.

● Abandoning water courses, the **grey heron** ventures onto meadows in winter to hunt small rodents.

Hen harrier (male)

Skylarks

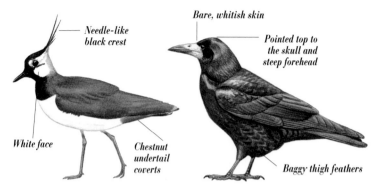

Needle-like
black crest

White face

Chestnut
undertail
coverts

Bare, whitish skin

Pointed top to
the skull and
steep forehead

Baggy thigh feathers

● In lowland areas, large flocks of **lapwings** frequent fields in the winter. The black and white plumage of this species, less bright at this time of year, is particularly visible in flight.

● From November onwards, the British **rook** population is swollen by birds arriving from Eastern Europe. The bare and whitish base of the bill distinguishes this species from the carrion crow.

● The **hooded crow** appears in small numbers every winter in southern and eastern Britain. It has characteristic grey and black plumage.

Skylarks

Carrion crow

● In winter, birds of prey, such as the hen harrier and merlin, hunt skylarks and finches.

● The **carrion crow**, which is resident in the open countryside all year round, readily forms flocks during the winter. Its plumage is black all over and its voice deeper that that of the rook.

Large Wading Birds

Herons, bitterns, cranes, egrets and flamingos differ from other birds by their large size, as well as by their long necks and legs. They are generally found in damp habitats, with the flamingo particularly associated with brackish coastal waters.

White plumage

Yellow feet

Black bill

● The **little egret**, a small, elegant white heron, usually fishes in shallow water.

Grey heron

Pale grey head and neck

● The **crane** is distinguished from the grey heron by its heavy build and bushy tail.

White underparts

Red patch (adult)

White patch

Black head and neck

● **Crane** in flight: neck outstretched, digitate wing tips.

Wholly grey body

Crane

● In winter, **herons** lose their black crest. Their plumage is grey above and whitish beneath.

Bushy tail

● **Heron** in flight: neck making an 'S', smooth wings.

● **Cattle egrets** are common around the Mediterranean. They often feed among horses and other grazing animals.

Yellowish bill

White plumage

Black feet

Smaller and more compact than the little egret

● The decorative black and red colours on the wings of the **greater flamingo** are mainly visible in flight.

● Cranes usually spend the winter around the Mediterranean, but some settle around large lakes further north.

Cranes

In flight, the neck and legs are outstretched

Neck held in an 'S'

Pink patch on the wing

● **Flamingos** are resident all year round in southern Spain and the Camargue. During the winter they spread to other parts of the Mediterranean coastline.

Heavy pink bill with a black tip

Long pink legs

Mediterranean Area

Areas bordering the Mediterranean are the regular winter quarters for some European birds such as the serin, blackcap and chiffchaff. In some years, swallows also stay here in small numbers.

● During the winter, **black redstart** (male above) live in western Europe, especially around the Mediterranean.

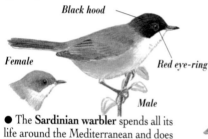

Black hood

Female

Red eye-ring

Male

● The **Sardinian warbler** spends all its life around the Mediterranean and does not move north for the summer.

Black cap

Grey cheeks and nape

Male

● **Blackcaps** overwinter in large numbers around the Mediterranean. The female is grey with a red-brown crown.

Yellow head

Small, conical bill

● The **serin**, a small finch from the Mediterranean area, breeds now throughout central Europe. It mainly overwinters around the Mediterranean.

Yellow rump

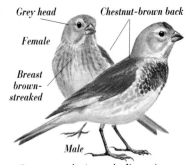

Grey head

Chestnut-brown back

Female

Breast brown-streaked

Male

● Summer and winter, the **linnet** is common in open countryside, farmland and lowland heath. The male has a grey head and bright red forehead and breast.

Dingy greenish-brown plumage

● In autumn, most **chiffchaffs** migrate south and west to winter around the Mediterranean.

Dark bill and legs

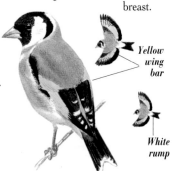

Yellow wing bar

White rump

● **Goldfinches** live in small flocks for the whole winter. The red and white mask and the yellow wing bar are characteristic.

● The **crag martin** is the only member of the swallow family to overwinter regularly in southern Europe. The other species do so only occasionally.

Crag martin

Birds of Prey

Birds of prey (raptors) like the sparrowhawk, which feeds on birds, or the buzzard and kestrel, which eat small mammals, find it easy to survive in temperate Europe in wintertime. On the other hand, raptors which eat insects, such as the honey buzzard, have to go to Africa for the winter to avoid dying of starvation.

● The **sparrowhawk**, normally a woodland bird, hawks for small birds around villages in the wintertime.

Female

Underparts with grey bars

Male

Underparts with chestnut-brown bars

● The **red kite** is a raptor with a slow, majestic flight and deeply forked tail. The body is bright chestnut.

White patch

● A typical **buzzard** is brown with a white crescent on its breast.

Male

Grey tail with a black bar

● A **kestrel** can be recognised from afar when it hovers over its prey. The male has a grey head.

Large head

Brown tail with a black bar

Female

● A female **kestrel** has plumage barred and streaked with black. Its tail ends in a broad black bar.

Short, rounded tail

Wide, rounded wings

Black wing tips

Brown plumage

Cream head and shoulders

White rump

Female

Male

● In winter, the **marsh harrier** is most frequent in southern areas. The male has grey wings with black ends and a chestnut-brown back.

● The male **hen harrier** is pale grey. The female is brown with a white patch on the rump.

Everyone can watch birds.
However, this leisure activity
does involve having some
equipment and a good
knowledge of basic
techniques. Amateur
ornithologists, who enjoy
their birdwatching, will soon
also want the satisfaction of
helping birds survive the
winter and reproduce in
spring.

Birdwatching

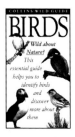

● A good **identification guide** is essential for recognising birds. Most books cover all birds that can be seen in Europe.

Identification is helped by making a sketch

The minimum items of equipment needed for birdwatching are binoculars, a bird book and a notebook. For watching birds in winter, a telescope and warm clothing are also often essential. In winter, many birds gather in large numbers on lakes (ducks), in bays and estuaries (waders), in fields (geese, lapwing) and even near houses (passerines), where they can easily be watched.

● A **field notebook** is the birdwatcher's memory. Basic details to note are: weather conditions, date, place, species seen and the number of individual birds.

● Birds can be watched even in very bad weather during the winter. Just settle comfortably at a window and watch sparrows and tits busy around the houses.

● Slow movements are less likely to frighten birds.

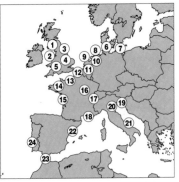

● With a **telescope** it is possible to watch birds from a great distance. You are less likely to disturb the birds. If they do get disturbed, they will fly off.

● The **tripod** for a telescope has to be quite heavy so that it is stable and wind resistant.

● The map below shows the best winter birdwatching sites in western Europe.

● Top of the range **binoculars** are much the most comfortable for protracted bird-watching. However, they are also the most expensive.

● The quality of cheap **binoculars** has improved considerably in the last few years.

1- Morecombe Bay
2- Mersey Estuary
3- Humber Flats
4- Ouse Washes
5- Severn Estuary
6- Waddenzee (Schleswig-Holstein)
7- Hiddensee
8- Waddenzee (Niedersäcksisches)
9- Waddenzee (Friesland, Holland)
10- Flevoland Polder
11- Rhine Estuary (Zeeland)
12- Straits of Dover
13- Baie de la Somme
14- Baie du Mont-Saint-Michel
15- Baie de l'Aiguillon, the Vendée, Ile de Ré and Ile d'Oléron
16- Lacs du Der and Lac de la forêt d'Orient

17- Lake Geneva
18- Camargue
19- Grado and Marano Lagoons
20- Po Delta, Venice Lagoon
21- Lac de Lesina
22- Ebro Delta
23- Guadalquivir Delta
24- Tagus Estuary

● In winter, ducks and geese can easily be watched by groups.

How to Identify Birds

To identify birds it is important to have a good understanding of their structure so that the coloured parts of their plumage can be correctly placed. The shape of the bill, presence of wing bars, or the way they perch or swim are other important features to note.

Greylag goose

Heavy build

Large, pale, conical bill

Neck

● Bill and leg colour is of prime importance in identifying geese. These features need to be checked under various light conditions.

Rump   *Back*   *Nape*   *Crown*

Tail feathers   *Bill*

Cheek

Breast

Wing feathers

Flank

Wing bar   *Belly*

Greenfinch

Great spotted woodpecker

Great tit   *Nuthatch*

● Birds do not all perch the same way. Tits behave like acrobats, finches prefer a flat surface, nuthatches perch upside-down and woodpeckers use their stiff tails as a support.

● When swimming, water birds have distinctive silhouettes which are useful in identification. From left to right: pochard, little grebe, cormorant, coot, mallard and great crested grebe.

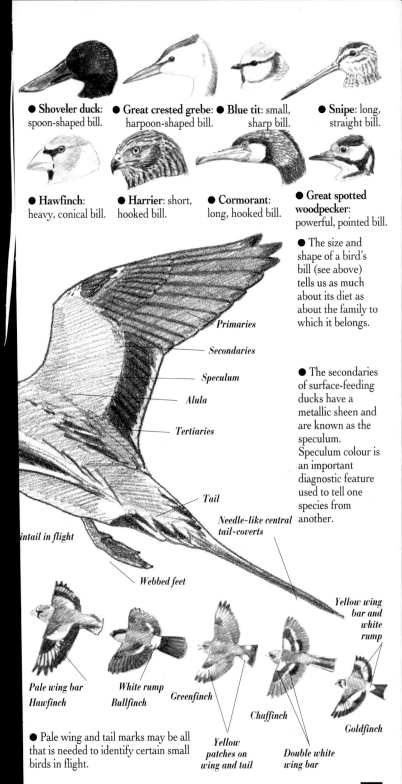

● **Shoveler duck:** spoon-shaped bill.

● **Great crested grebe:** harpoon-shaped bill.

● **Blue tit:** small, sharp bill.

● **Snipe:** long, straight bill.

● **Hawfinch:** heavy, conical bill.

● **Harrier:** short, hooked bill.

● **Cormorant:** long, hooked bill.

● **Great spotted woodpecker:** powerful, pointed bill.

● The size and shape of a bird's bill (see above) tells us as much about its diet as about the family to which it belongs.

● The secondaries of surface-feeding ducks have a metallic sheen and are known as the speculum. Speculum colour is an important diagnostic feature used to tell one species from another.

Primaries

Secondaries

Speculum

Alula

Tertiaries

Tail

Needle-like central tail-coverts

intail in flight

Webbed feet

Yellow wing bar and white rump

Pale wing bar
Hawfinch

White rump
Bullfinch

Greenfinch

Chaffinch

Goldfinch

● Pale wing and tail marks may be all that is needed to identify certain small birds in flight.

Yellow patches on wing and tail

Double white wing bar

Survival in Winter

Great tit

Birds have to eat more in winter in order to win the struggle against the cold. However, the drop in temperature, snow on the ground, fewer hours of daylight and shortage of some food sources are additional obstacles birds have to overcome in order to find enough to eat. Each species has its own strategy for survival in winter.

● Certain birds (eg. tits) which are primarily insectivorous in the summer, eat seed in winter.

● The blue tit is very skilled at finding **caterpillars**.

Caterpillar

Spider

● **Insects** and **spiders** are food for many birds in summer.

Aphid

● Many insectivorous birds (warblers, swallows) fly south to spend winter under the warmer skies of Africa. In late summer, **swallows** can be seen gathering on telephone wires before they set off.

● **Seeds** and **dried fruit**, which are high in calories, are very popular with birds in wintertime.

Walnut

Hazel nut

Beech mast (beech nuts)

● Birds find food more easily when they are in a flock.

Chaffinch and brambling

Greenfinch

● A **great tit** feeds nine chicks, only one of which will reach one year old.

● During the winter months, bird mortality is very high, especially among the inexperienced juveniles.

● Studies have shown that nearly 87% of great tits die in the first year of life and that 49% of adult birds disappear every year.

Robin

● To combat the cold, birds fluff up their plumage, trapping an insulating layer of air under their feathers.

● Contrary to what is commonly believed, birds suffer more in winter from shortage of food than from the cold.

● Birds which feed far out at sea, like this **guillemot**, may die during violent winter storms.

● In winter, tits and finches look for food near houses and are sometimes followed by **sparrowhawks** which hunt them.

Feeding Birds

Small birds appreciate the supplement to their diet when food is put out in winter. Even if the impact on their survival rates is small, feeding offers an ideal opportunity to watch tits, finches and other birds under excellent conditions.

● Block of lard and sunflower seed.

● Covered bird table: traditional model popular with **finches**.

Fieldfare

Redwing

● Half a coconut shell to hang from a branch.

● Bird seed mix.

● Berry-bearing shrubs (eg rowan and spindle) attract blackbirds and thrushes.

● Peanuts and hazel nuts can be put out in a net with coarse mesh. Do not give salted nuts.

● **Robins** come and pick up crumbs.

● Milk and salt may kill birds. Do not put them out.

● Birds like sunflower seeds best of all.

● When there is snow on the ground, gardens where bird food is put out are soon invaded by many different species.

● Small nets filled with fat or seeds can be hung from branches for tits and **nuthatches** (as illustrated).

● A block of wood drilled with large holes filled with lard may attract the **great spotted woodpecker**.

● In winter, birds need to drink and bathe. Fresh water left out in a shallow saucer and frequently changed, will provide drink and bath for birds like these house sparrows.

● Apples left on the ground will attract **blackbirds** and **starlings**.

Getting Ready for Spring

Winter is the perfect season for constructing and putting up nesting boxes for birds. In extremely cold weather, nest boxes may be used for shelter during the night. Then, when spring comes, birds will build their nests in these, by now familiar, artificial holes. Depending on the species that you hope to attract, various kinds of nest boxes can be built. For all models, plywood or rough-sawn planks should be chosen and the box should definitely not be treated with chemicals.

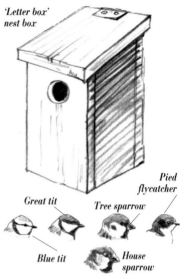

'Letter box' nest box

Pied flycatcher

Great tit

Tree sparrow

Blue tit

House sparrow

● The '**letter box**' design is very suitable for tits and pied flycatchers. Fix on a tree trunk 2–5m above the ground. Dimensions: L=15cm, W=15cm, H=25cm, entrance hole diameter=25–30mm.

L: length
W: width
H: height

Half box nest box

Flycatcher

● A **half box**, fixed on a wall in a quiet place 2–4m above the ground is suitable for grey wagtail and spotted flycatcher and may be adopted by black redstart.
Dimensions: L=15cm, W=12cm, H=16–20cm, entrance hole=8 x 15cm.

The entrance hole must be off-centre

Large opening nest box

Black redstart

● Specially designed for black redstart and redstart, the **large opening nest box** should be fixed to a wall 2–3m above the ground, preferably facing the garden.
Dimensions: L=30cm, W=20cm, H=20cm, entrance hole=9 x 9cm.

● A clear place on a trunk of a tall tree makes a suitable site for a letter box style nest box.

● Never use nails on trees: it is a good idea to fix the boxes with plastic-coated electric flex.

Swift

● A **nest box for a swift** should be fixed under high eaves. Dimensions: L=25cm, W=15cm, H=13cm, entrance hole=4 x 6cm.

● Prefabricated house martin nests can be fixed against the front of houses.

House martin

Nest box for a swift

● Bird boxes compensate for the loss of old hollow trees.

Nest box for a house martin

Nest box for a grey wagtail

Nest box for a black redstart

● Boxes will be more successful if they are not sited into prevailing winds and rain. They should be

'Letter box' nest box

sheltered from the sun and tilted slightly forwards.

● Like many hole-nesting birds, **great tits** take to 'letter box' style nest boxes.

● Old buildings abound in holes where birds can build nests. Modern homes are too weathertight: nest boxes make up for the lack of holes.

Great tit

Glossary

•ARCTIC
Describes places (and species) around the North Pole.

•BRACKISH
Brackish water is a mixture of fresh and salt water. Water in estuaries and lagoons is brackish.

•BREEDING PLUMAGE
Plumage worn during the breeding season.

•COVERTS
Small feathers covering the base of the wing and tail.

•DIGITATE
Describes a bird's wing when the feathers spread out at the tip like fingers.

•FINCH
Name for birds in the Fringillidae family: chaffinch, brambling, serin, siskin, linnet, greenfinch, hawfinch, etc.

•HONKING
Describes the call of a goose.

•INSECTIVOROUS
Describes a bird which feeds on insects.

•MIGRATION
Journey made by a bird each autumn between its breeding and wintering grounds and the reverse journey made in spring. Birds which migrate are called migratory birds.

•MORPHOLOGY
Study of the external shape.

•MOULT
Term for the replacement of old feathers by new ones once or twice a year.

•MUD BANK/FLAT
Muddy area exposed by the sea at low tide.

•ORNITHOLOGIST
Someone who studies birds.

•PASSERINE
Name for birds in the Passiformes order: larks, finches, crows, thrushes, starlings etc. They are also called perching birds and song birds.

•PLUMAGE
A bird's feathers.

•RAPTOR
A bird of prey, eg sparrowhawk, buzzard, kestrel.

•RESIDENT
A resident bird remains all year in the same area: it does not migrate.

•SPECULUM
Wing feathers (secondaries) which, in surface-feeding ducks, have a metallic sheen.

•STUBBLE
Fields where the base of the stalk is left after a cereal crop has been harvested.

•TERRITORIAL
Describes a bird which defends its territory, that is, the area in which it finds food, shelter and nesting site.

•WADERS

A group of medium-sized birds with long legs and bills which feed by probing damp mud: eg, curlew, snipe and redshank.

•WING BAR

A coloured band across the wing, visible when the wing is both open and closed.

Further Reading

Collins Watch Guide Birds of the Countryside, HarperCollins, London, 1997

Couzens D, *Wings Guide to British Birds*, HarperCollins, London 1997

Flegg J, *Collins Gem Birds Photoguide*, HarperCollins, London, 1995

Heinzel H, Fitter R and Parslow R, *Collins Pocket Guide Birds of Britain and Europe with North Africa and the Middle East*, HarperCollins, London, 1996

Holden P, *Collins Wild Guide Birds*, HarperCollins, London, 1996

Singer D, *Collins Nature Guide Garden Birds*, HarperCollins, London, 1996

Soper T, *The New Bird Table Book*, David and Charles

Addresses

Royal Society for the Protection of Birds
The Lodge
Sandy
Bedfordshire SG19 2DL

Young Ornithologists Club (YOC)
The Lodge
Sandy
Bedfordshire SG19 2DL

The British Trust for Ornithology
The Nunnery
Thetford
Norfolk AP24 2PU

Scottish Ornithologists Club (SOC)
21 Regent Terrace
Edinburgh EH7 5BT

Index

Picture Credits